LEAF RAKER

the

LEAF RAKER

a collection of poems

V.T. Abercrombie

Mae S. Barclay

Simone Bateman

Mary Esther Bintliff

Elizabeth Bratten

Mary Louise Ferguson

Reba Gloger

Sally Hubbard

Mary Hurter

Lucille Joy

Vassar Miller

Cathy Stern

Helen Williams

BROWN RABBIT PRESS

ACKNOWLEDGEMENTS

"Winter Walk" by V.T. Abercrombie was first printed in *riverSedge*. "Three Middle-Aged Widows" by Simone Bateman is reprinted with permission from *Voices: The Art and Science of Psychotherapy,* Summer 1980, Vol. 16, No. 2. "Entre Nous" by Mary Louise Ferguson first appeared in a *Book of the Year,* Poetry Society of Texas. "Assertion" by Vassar Miller first appeared in *Kaleidoscope.* "The Kashgar" by Helen Williams first appeared in *North Country.*

Portraits by Lucille Joy

Cover illustration by Simone Bateman

Design and production by Mae S. Barclay

Library of Congress Catalog Card Number 83-072276
ISBN 0-933988-03-6

Brown Rabbit Press
31 Briar Hollow
Houston, Texas 77027

for Terry Doody

CONTENTS

CONTENTS

REFLECTIONS

Hey old friend, I see a movement there, an
ear point, a whisk of tail, beyond the mirrored glass.

I remember, at ten, how I used to play, at words, patting
them in round to watch them roll—extravagant statements

to my Catholic grandmother—"Grandmere, I would die for
you . . . for mother . . . for Jesus . . ." Not a flicker of you then.

In my twenties you were much mentioned. I carted philosophies
about like kittens held by their loose neck skin

never noticing your eye reflected in the glass of my
wedding picture or in the shine of my new Revere pots.

Occasionally, in those years, you left prints
on my kitchen counter. I washed them off with Ajax.

Days on days of mops and wax made crescents in the corners
of my kitchen floor. You left a whisker there, where

you stalked uncle Herve, playing him awhile—
Later pouncing on my mother.

Don't Cheshire me, behind my new stainless steel
double door refrigerator, your teeth left punctures

when I had hepatitis. Are you there, old feline, gathering
reflections, in a micro-wave oven door, a bright spatula or

in the toaster's sheen, where we'll be face to face,
your face mirror image to mine?

V. T. Abercrombie

SONNET TO HUSBANDS

In the mornings I make breakfast. My tools,
no longer bridal-bright, (The teflon nicked,
the fork is bent, the handles burnt like spools
without thread.) serve our needs. Filtered and thick—
I pour devotions of coffee without
sugar and cream. With eggs, bread, and bacon,
sausage or ham, I can create, set out,
a fine dish. My hands, in incantation,
move over the sink. Lines of script on my
palms read "The way to a man's heart . . . Making
marriage work . . .". Faucet on, I rinse and dry.
The toast is browned, the eggs are simmering.
    Now it's time to assemble the food, take
    my spatula, load my life on your plate.

V. T. Abercrombie

FALL/YOU

You are like the leaves covering the pond,
full-colored, curled and crowded roses,
solid as though to walk on.

Leaves, immobile, sheeted
on the pond, whisper enticements,
promises of stability.

Tomorrow the pond will clear,
exchange an autumn flash
for the substance of your shadow.

WINTER WALK

Winter's frigid air clicks along
behind my heels
tapping the way without a stick.
Sounds come back again
echoing off limestone rocks.
At the bottom of the hill
just around the curve,
a deer is dead.
Fur intact, head to the side,
the eyes seem to see
past the wind
that swallows sound.

V. T. Abercrombie

GRANDMOTHER'S HOUSE

The rose garden at mere's house
was a circle with two entrances,
a druids' circle, a fairy ring,
a bed, kept weedless like marriage,
to be tended, sprinkled with water
and religion. The roses stayed my
same height with petals soft-slick
and malleable that I pulled, closed

like a pillow in my palm and popped.

The zoo was close to mere's house.
Lions called out at night, captive
roars to African lion gods whose
powers were never meant to breach
oceans and chain link fences. Their
sounds, rippled skin and muscle
tissue, overlayed the smell of roses,
gave choice to night and childhood.

V.T. Abercrombie

FOR PAT

We talked and never talked.
I never told you about the clock
unheard, that ticked and moved
sounds of time—its current
constant in my life.
My delusion—the sameness
of our bodies, eyes, hands,
humaness, mutterings of time.

You filled a tub with time
and let it fill you up.
Anticipation, limp and sodden,
barriers of smiles, yellow hair
lacking Ophelia's flowers—
like that water, dissolver
of spirit, drains, has
drained, will drain away.

Somewhere along the twenty
years since your death,
I've lost the sound of time.
Eternity's no longer wound,
but digital. Imagine
the face of that digital
clock, summer-lightning-lit,
racing our numbers through the sky.

V. T. Abercrombie

DOCTOR'S APPOINTMENT

Mother, mother, mother, repeats
your name, reminds us who you are.
Here, in the doctor's office, you
present yourself, old breasts bared,
your conversation loose with age.
I remember your tales of my passage
down the birth canal. Today your eyes
puzzle my features like a newborn face.
You hold in your chemistry
certain memories—speech patterns,
children banging the screen door,
picking mayhaws by the river.
Your mind, like a slippery baby,
came down, not in painful surges,
but effortlessly, like the tears
that constantly course your face,
leaving you a spillage of memories
among milk-eyed strangers.

V. T. Abercrombie

THE CHAIR

It was always there, blue speckled,
blocky, called an "Easy Chair".
My father's chair. Company, steered
past it, sat on other furniture.
They said his ankles were bad—
youthful injuries—said he'd been

a quarterback, a star. Couldn't
do what he wanted to because of
them. Sidelined, he sat its
cushions, drink in hand. When
the drink was gone he would tap
on the table next to the chair,

with the empty glass, and mama
would bring him another. The night
of words loud like cheers,
like the sound of a crowd,
like bones snapping, he stood up
and threw the chair across the room

end over end, over end, over end,
its shadow trailing silence.
When he died I dreamed the
chair—cartwheeling soft as a loss,
hewing air like a football, caught,
and put back where it belonged.

V. T. Abercrombie

FLIGHT 127 DEPARTURE TIME: 8:09

All the emotional things have been said;
The words are neatly packed away in your carry-on mind
For you to contemplate later.

But your eyes are shining into mine,
Darker than I have ever seen them.
Your voice, rough with caring,
Speaks of times and places, schedules, miles.

Too soon
The dream-whip clouds erase your plane.
I try to remember how you look.

BAROMETER

The orange-red stars
Scattered on my patio
Tell me that spring has gone,
And summer's here.

I think I'll send the weatherman
A small pomegranate tree.

Mae S. Barclay

PRAYER

Keep this day gentle for my love.
If he thinks of me, let him smile;
Wrap him in a warming glow
Of quiet contentment.

Give him the strength to win
Today's important battles;
Lift him above small irritations,
Heal his wounds, put his mind at ease.

Fill his mind with dreams
So he will reach
Toward a special star
That guides his destiny.

Bless him with all the joys
Of being loved and loving.
Protect him from all hurt and grief;
Keep this day gentle for my love.

Mae S. Barclay

PLUM TREE

The bare boughs of my plum tree
Zigzag across the sky.
Knots of cocoons stutter
Along the smooth dark branches,
Swollen with unborn blossoms.

A few brave petals
Drift in the sunlight,
Snowsuited children tired of winter's wraps,
Running to greet spring.

NURSING HOME

Gnarled hands reach,
Grasp at passers-by .
Antiseptic air is filled with whispers:
"Take me home . . . take me home . . ."

An unsteady swish, squeak
Moves wheelchairs tentatively
Down long bare corridors,
Each passenger grimly determined
To make the trip, once more,
To nowhere . . .

Mae S. Barclay

PEGGY

Her dying took a long time.
A fog spread over our lives. Time was cloud-heavy,
And our faces were strained with surface smiles.
Days darkened; her moods grew stormy.
We watched her too closely as awareness distanced her,
Brittling her voice.

Slowly grief nibbled at the card-structures of our lives,
Testing the strength of love.

Now, in the aftermath, we are still
Picking through the debris of her life . . . sorting, sorting,
Grasping fragments.

I miss her. I feel pain, not knowing
If it is hers or mine.

Mae S. Barclay

AT LAST I STAND UPON MY FATHER'S LAND

The vineyards, climbing high into the hills,
Start at the river's edge. Gnarled trunks
Twist into tender vines, giving no hint
Of the rich bounty to come.
Towering eucalyptus trees backdrop the castle,
Where time has left its whispers in the walls.
From its juncture with the Rhine,
The Mozelle curls through narrow canyons,
Snakes around towns of timbered houses,
Foams and fights its way to Koblenz and to Tier,
The tortured city where Caesar Augustine bathed in blood.

This was my father's land . . . a land of fruit and flowers,
Where life was good, and children, spellbound by elders' tales,
Lived peaceful lives and played at emperors and wars.
There was a sound of centuries in the air,
A pride in past survivals, conquests, gains.

My father kept a sense of history all his days;
He loved the land, its beauty and its gifts.
His Germany became our fantasy,
And threads of Tier were woven through our lives.

Mae S. Barclay

AN INDIAN RHINO WAS GALLOPING

toward Ctesias, the Greek physician.
At the hasty sound of the hooves, Ctesias
anticipated seeing a horse.
Instead, to his amazement,
he was confronted by a Unicorn,
a unicorned horse!
Ctesias' face was radiant with elation!
Enlivened by the reception, our rhino
attempted to repeat the miracle.
The rest of the day, horn high,
legs lengthened to their ultimate,
a grid of muscles fastened to his body,
he approached every passerby,
to his surprise, with increasing success.
At the end of the day, ego uplifted
in a supernatural lust of joy,
he reached a pond and bent over it.
From the depths of the water's sandy bed,
horn high, eyes as star sapphires,
legs grounded on dainty hooves,
an exquisite figure emerged
and gave him an accolade of welcome
into the mythical kingdom of the Unicorns.

Simone Bateman

TO A FRIEND

Well, you lost him to a school teacher!
He must have been looking for some order in his life,
but don't worry, he'll come back;
after all, he did not take a lover, but a wife!

Marriage is an honorable institution
where each cultivates the other's mediocrity.
Seldom the union evolves into a higher standard,
but too often sinks for the sake of sanctity.

Go, grow, let lovers come and go!
Later there will be a time
when a husband will be fine!

SANCTIMONIOUS GOODY-NESS

In New York with pompous dignity
the apostle of Jesus over zealously
launches Carlo Gambino to heaven
brooding on Nixon's amorality with disdain.

In New York the apostle of Jesus
is becoming as rich as Croesus.

Simone Bateman

THREE

middle-aged widows
enter the cemetery.

The first one,
pale, eyes lost in blue mascara,
brings a plant of yellow chrysanthemums,
a tribute to their sunny days.

The second,
of sturdy physique but shy aspect,
drags on rollers a green plant
twice her size,
fearing that he might rise again.

But the third,
light as a dancer,
balances in each hand
a dandelion and a wild strawberry plant
to entice rabbits and birds
to keep him company,
for life had uprooted the past.

Simone Bateman

GRANDFATHER

Handsome beyond comparison excepting my son,
his eyes, two dots of sky before pollution,
dreamed only of man's paradise
and his hair was sun-disguised.
Grandfather was a leader of the Commune
and by men and women equally idolized.
The first blindly embraced his cause,
welcoming the consequences;
the ground around him, enriched by human sacrifice,
was vibrant with heroic feats
and the world was sanctified.
Women devoted to the living
proudly bore his genes,
securing for the future
the fruits of his daring heart.
When he was captured by his adversaries
grandmother dressed as a nun,
visited the jail, a pot of water in hand,
retrieved the unfaithful, hiding him under her skirt,
and saved him from the six o'clock firing squad.
But Nature, which longs for balance
and winters to protect her seed's vitality,
touched grandfather's head with a sunray
when, hatless, he accompanied
the body of a friend to the cemetery.
That night, at the banquet for the deceased,
laughing at happy memories,
grandfather died,
his eyes fixed forever on man's paradise.

Simone Bateman

GRANDMOTHER

A fact it was for all, had the queen of England
walked beside her, the ovations
would have been directed to grandmother.
She carried her soul high and tall
                                        chin up
Wife to an unconstant husband but political idol,
she had to share his attentions with many.
When her sister died giving birth
to grandfather's child,
she made him hers and one with her own eleven
                                        chin up
She worked overtime covering five continents
with her flowers made of ribbons
for the ladies' shoulders, corsets, pillows.
Grandfather turned them
into pamphlets, bullets, regrets
but all for the workers, promise of better days.
Silent, she complied
                                        chin up
But one day grandfather died.
Gently and lady-like
she picked up her skirt, ankle high,
and over the conventional line stepped and sinned
with the young man next door.
She immersed herself in a pool of love,
laughed the city sounds away, and
cut in the air
a jungle of bright-colored silhouettes
of her past, present and future,
to encircle the domain
where she was sole to reign
                                        chin up.

Simone Bateman

DINGALING

Dingaling, Ding Dong.
Bells on their trucks,
the cement workers
drive down the street
to empty their whirling barrels
into a man-made pit,
where soon will be erected
a high-rise condominium.

> Jesus, compassion awakened
> by the sound of the bells,
> comes to remit the sins
> of the lepers' hell!

Now, freed from their cargo,
the truck drivers return home
with an airy feeling
of cleansing.

> His need for compassion quenched,
> Jesus returns happy to His Father's land.

Simone Bateman

AGE

is the symbol for the space between you and the end,
approximate evaluation of the state of your vessel,
and the factual extension between illusions
and expectations.

Aging is a monk's acceptance of the Order,
an astronomer's observation of the course of the stars,
Nature's irreversible verdict to your body.

But the mind's source of energy
owes little to time or fact.
The substance of its vortex does not decay;
only the brain ceases to decipher.

With the coming of my autumn,
like leaves my expectations cover my daily walk;
but the wings of my dreams are not clipped
and my ageless mind take from, and gives to, life.

Simone Bateman

JOY IS THIS

Sky vanilla and blue
Joy is hip high
In a turquoise sea
Alongside the heaving
Circle of porpoises
Nosey and corpulent
Closer more porpoises
Scatter enormous
Aquamarines
Grinning grinning
They break out of school
There's no recess
No king's ex
I'm
It

Mary Esther Bintliff

SONS AND LOVERS

As we walk the mile to the edge
Of the sidewalk and I am earnestly
Pointing out the directions
I will wonder
Were they explicit
As turning a corner you encounter
Someone, somewhere, perhaps
A stranger
Will you know the look they give you
The look of my camera eyes
For I have passed you secretly
In time and again it will take
My life to untangle
This jungle of grief left in my hands
I have sewn myself shut inside
Your eyelids
Curled myself in your head
To cradle and rock you
Disturbing a balance of safety
Measured impossibly
"Hurry up it's time"
I will mourn all the days
I do not hold you
Mourn now the before
And after leavetaking
To practise repair of the damage
I construct a day away from the phone
Make four appointments, break two
Memorize stains on the wall
Wash my hair twice before evening
Cut if off before dawn
Comfort me the while longer
Given time

Mary Esther Bintliff

Enough it will be easy
Lie if you must
Sabotage becomes you
Close your eyes and forget me
Never forget what I taught you
Tell me what you regret
Go on

ON MORA STREET

He sat
Crosslegged
In the naked wind
Cloaked with vermin
Laced with air
Holding a cup
Of evening gloom
Opening his panes
Of crystal silk
I gaze reflecting
In sockets of milk
And above his head
Like an onyx brooch
Fastened—unfastened
About to fall
The black moth clung
And clawed its own
Shadow on the wall
In the haunting
"Don't forget me"
Dreams
I promised

Mary Esther Bintliff

BLACK MAGIC

Brown butter won't melt
The face so tender
They hid my sword
But I kept the shiv
Used it to pick
My brains at night
Yank off my crown
Watch me
Whip out another
Crack my jaw and I'll
Open it wider
Spitting out wads
Of humble pie

Thunderbolts ripple
Across my shoulders
Lightning strikes
From my arms extended
Mountains confused
With boulders crumble
Quietly shattered
Between my thighs

I am
The leader of your
Third world order
Call me outrageous
Hypnotizer
Call me a liar
Change my name
I'm Ali
Cool black
The rumbler
It's Saturday night
And I'm
King

Mary Esther Bintliff

THE WARLOCK

One afternoon when I was young
In a village no one seems to remember
The morning of fiesta
With convent bells tolling the hills
Dogs barking heard so they say
As far away as Michoacan
With the dust in the square watered down
We waited laughing and tittering
Laced in frills fluttering like tissue
Eating whirled cotton candy
Circling clockwise the square
Bordered in blatant hues of hibiscus
Bougainvillia frangipani
Watching, the clash of colored satin
Strangely right on the gypsies
Snaking their wrists now in a sinuous
Clicking of castanets and tambourines
Jingling silver coins in glass bottles

As if signalled someone stepped on a dog
The band tuned up and the day
Began in a wave of dancing

One gypsy unlike the others tall
copper-chested with a shine like
New money spun on his feet laughing
I watched in a dream
All around there was shouting
More feet than shoes
Wine than glasses
Kissed lips
With a stopped sun overhead
A magician in black conjured
Live doves with a broken wand
And a tweak of the glove
One dropped at my feet

Mary Esther Bintliff

A froth of twisted white
Crepe paper

And there was the gypsy standing alone
He turned his head
Green eyes topaz flecked
Mocked me
He had expected me
Keeping his eyes on mine he poured
A glass of golden wine and surely
Placed it before me
I glanced from his eyes to the wine
In it the sun shone small a gold coin
People looked like hulled nuts
Mountains shrank into pebbles
Houses were snuff boxes flung
About the square a black cape
Unloosed a white dove upside down
In that golden glass held afternoon
Mesmerized by those eyes time hung
In a gulp I drank down

Boys girls mariachis dogs doves gypsies
Rolled down my throat
The music glugged once and was gone
Gone I tell you
Nothing more moved or happened
I was alone

I tried to wish back the village
Sick of the wine to free the dove
And the music
I never could
Never did

Mary Esther Bintliff

Somewhere in my body there lies
A fiesta
Ribboned dogs balloons children dancing
And a gypsy who dropped his eyes
To my glass asking me to work wonders

Even now I want to see him
Come through the woods
Bringing mystery and enchantment
His eyes telling me to undream myself
Believe in a dove made of air
Circling overhead
I have a lifetime to find him
He moves in the crystal

APPLES

Look at them
Sly—happy
A lapful
Of apples
All cousins
With similar
Smiles
Oh Adam
Green Adam
You hadn't a prayer
Did it have to be
Waiting round
Like a Monday
Ripe as a kiss
So many sunny
Red apples
There

Mary Esther Bintliff

TOWARD GRANADA

Once in Spain
I saw along the side of a mountain
A ledge holding a child's village.
Spun-sugar dwellings
With cinnamon roofs
Doors of yellow, red, and blue
Drew in the sun.
Accordion stairs
                    let
                        down

To meet the hooves
Of toy donkeys carrying wood.
The road
            dropped then
                                to common clay

Olive groves with cork trees between.
When I looked up,
The prismatic light had faded,
To somber green
And rain.

Elizabeth Bratten

HARVEST

As I lift the apple to cut away the skin
That which I have lost
Attends

As I lay open the fruit, cutting into the core
Seed-star in the heart
That which I have lost
Extends

Recalling the spring and the bud
The falling away of the flower
The orchard bare on the hill
The encompassing snow.

Elizabeth Bratten

CHOSEN

I had no choice in the catch;
Hand over hand, fish of the heart
Was drawn into the boat,
A frenzied flip-flop as liquid silver
Pooled, congealed and set.
Dead eye talked me to the well
To wash my hands, to wash away
The salt.
In the cool that opens morning,
From the well that keeps the memory
Fresh, I washed, out of my childhood,
Out of my life, out of my mind,
I washed, that I come out new,
Closed mouth still
Where the little red runs out.

Elizabeth Bratten

RED

We were led into the red heart and there we saw a man
laid out in a black suit and a red tie as if he had
been called, untimely, from an affair of state.
His skin was yellow as the teeth of an old tiger.
His left hand was open, curved as a hand might curve,
naturally, the right, a clenched fist.

We shuffled through the vault in silence, the guards
were grim and ready to stifle any sound or gesture.
Crowded against the marble walls of the crypt, we moved
in an endless file that began at dawn and ended at dusk,
circling the core of light that poured over the bier.

We climbed from the tomb and came to the square,
to the open of melting snow, to monuments of war,
where the young are tutored to remember what the old
could not forget. Above us, the red star in the
freezing sky,

Beyond the walls, miles upon mile upon mile,
the birches, the snow.

Elizabeth Bratten

LAST LIGHT

In the ending of that summer
Drawn shutters held back the sun.
Cicadas hummed in black oaks
As in other summers.
In that year
With the first leaf of fall
All wicker was covered,
Cushions to the wall.
Lemons, limes, cherries, peaches,
And plums,
Luster of summer shimmered,
And kettles turned.
Siftings of radiance rung down,
Going as all summers go
To earth, to jar, to faded gown
And empty swing,
Last light on soft beat of wings
Flickering low.

Elizabeth Bratten

THE WEDDING GUESTS

The notes of the recessional muffled the minister's last
Words, "God be with you, and with you."

You drive north on the interstate. Down embankments in deep
Ravines, you leave the dogwood trapped; the white scarred
Petals drip, shrugging the last snow.

I fly west, conforming to the cinched belt, I lean and
Watch the clouds stretch, fresh cumulus, newly sprung,
Chaste as your open hands.

Our faces were cameos in bas relief, struck to validate
The import of that bright occasion; our hearts recede.
On the great concourses, earth and sky, we move, to resume

The proper level of our lives.

Elizabeth Bratten

THE SUN DOES NOT COME DOWN AS IT DID THEN

Blue-eyed sister, Momma's favorite doll, I unwrap the wadding
of years from around your quiet face. You stand before me
in your blue school jumper, white socks, and saddle oxfords, new
on the Brussels carpet. You give me a musing, thoughtful
look, wondering at your headstrong twin, so eager to play
next door. But you follow, as I push back the screen and run
downstairs. We walk out into the sunshine of that November afternoon.

I come home alone, and I hear a voice, that sounds like
my voice, calling, "Momma, Momma," at the foot of the stair.

I have walked those long white halls, counting each square;
the fumes of phenol burn my eyes. I have reached the last door,
uncounted times, and in the dim room the same nun draws the
curtain aside, and I wait at the edge of the white mountain
where I knew you were hiding, and whisper, "the game's over;
we must go home."

Elizabeth Bratten

LETTER FROM SLIM

Riding down Come Alive Ridge
after two weeks at Goat Basin
mending fence, pulling calves
and gathering strays, we found
the river belly deep to a horse.
At Juniper Flat, the whole pack
of ranch hounds came gangling
over the meadow and yapped us
through Cherry Canyon to first sight
of snow-capped Holt, twelve thousand feet
of purple in the last light.
Suppertime and the bell clanging.
We unsaddled in Y7 corral:
two cowpokes fit for the dipping vat,
and all thirty-seven hounds,
their bodies rifled at the moon.

Mary Louise Ferguson

THE WINTER PIT

"Begonias in bloom!" we laughed,
brushing the snow
from the heavy glass,
leaning together
to see the treasures below.

My grandmother
                had such an earthen room,
dug with her own hands
and covered with old windowpanes.
It made a magic hiding place
when summer came:
"To the dungeon!" we would cry,
and some chubby princess
would languish there
till dinner time.

In the swift days
of slanting sun,
our own grandchildren come
to see the wonder-show
of begonias in bloom
beneath the snow.

Mary Louise Ferguson

LANDSCAPE IN DRYPOINT

A child's lost boot
lay shriveled and bent
at the edge of the lane
where a hedge of sunflowers
promised fulfillment
over the hill.
Then I saw the Adobe,
squat, gray-brown and stark,
without a fence or tree.
Beyond, the mesa stretched southward
as lonely as a lump in the throat.
To this gaunt land,
detached from all but the horizon,
I came as a bride.

A sameness dyed the days
the color of the dust
on hat brims and brows
of shy cowhands.
Words were exchanged,
sparse and dry as the grass
when the riders returned from the range,
the last chores done.

Bedtime came at dusk
and the next passive light
meant morning.

Thirty years away.
the memory sleeps
beneath a blanket
of small talk and laughter.

Even the palm trees
                    whisper.

Mary Louise Ferguson

THE LEAF RAKER

A wooded ravine is a museum.
Leaves, especially the flame-colored,
should be preserved.
Reaching under the magnolia,
clearing the mound of fallen
yellow and brown, I can see
Mrs. Sommer, who lived alone on Sycamore,
our street, when I was young.
Everyone thought she was crazy,
the way she raked her yard every day,
raking, even in the wind.
She was tall and thin
and she and the rake and the trees
made a kind of ballet.

I can understand her raking,
her sweep of mind:
she may have had a poem
in the making.

Mary Louise Ferguson

ENTRE NOUS

A summer night has canny power
in its light-fingered touch
to reach inside the buttoned years
and dangle square before my eyes
a scar-seared, sutured thing.
The pretension of each tiny stitch,
entrenched in gristle now,
still sensitive to thistle-prick.
My sly pick-pocket friend,
you'll find no tapestry as rare
in the fairest Camelot
your entry may portend.
So June into July
while I retie a raveled knot
in a moment without end.

Mary Louise Ferguson

THE FOWLS CAME DOWN

— Genesis 15:11

Sailing
in spirals,
rising,
gliding
down the wind,
we wait to perform
our priestly
last rites.
Settling
on our scaly
reptilian legs,
we bow before
the coup de grace
on royal crown
or copperhead.
It is the mission
of all feathered black
hunchbacks.

Remember,
we were there
carving a dark halo
in the air
over Calvary.

Mary Louise Ferguson

ANIMAL TRAINER

My beasts lie quiet now,
no longer nervous at the antics of the clowns.
We sleep back to back
and they leap
through hoops of fire
without a crack of whip.
On rarest moonlit nights
their old vigor returns
and yearly they climb
the branches of the Christmas tree,
but I soothe them
with a naked hand.
Only the finale lacks perfection:
my gilded body
borne on their saffron backs,
the tips of my glittering boa
caught in their teeth,
we circle the arena.
The crowd rises.
The band strikes the first notes
of Auld Lang Syne
and the boa
constricts.

Mary Louise Ferguson

ROOSTER HERFORD

He was a skinny-butt
little old man
you could put half the county
in what was left over
in the seat of his britches
he didn't give a rat's ass
what the world thought
and he told it like it was
if I told you how old he was
I'd be lying
he was white-headed
long as I knowed him
when he put a ton fertilizer
on your truck
don't check
it wuz
he got along fine with farm wimmen
but he despised town wimmen
like poissen
crazy ole biddies
always wanting white eggs
never knew when to plant
TOMATOES
didn't know their ass
from a hole in the ground
there wasn't any love lost
they wuz always dodging
his tobacco juice
he lived in the back
of the feed store with eight cats
who didn't seem to mind him much
Monday morning
when the train came in
he was sorting shallots
he walked down to the depot
never came back

Reba Gloger

THE WIDOW

One pale potentate came
    full of gin and pomposity
another burly bed-hopper
    packed a forked tongue
if I had money, would travel.
    The thought of being lonely
drove almost to suicide.
    I have since bought dark glasses!
You have to kiss a lot of frogs
    before you find a prince.

OLD PECOS NIGHT

Against the adobe wall
I watch old stars break up
and fall out over the mesa
a hundred miles away.
Soon the wolves asleep on rocks
in far off canyons will rise
to call the moon.
Today the sage, grey and still,
stored the sun, and tonight,
blows back its breath
over the hills.

Reba Gloger

SECRETS

Long ago I stopped
Following
Small boys in crowds
But once I bought
A top and hid it
In a drawer with
Things that I forgot
Like that forbidden
Look at your
Dried apple face
That mixed up day
The scar no longer
Hurts but sometimes
On windy days
When small boys with
Kites puncture
The sky
I Wonder Which
One is you

Reba Gloger

BLACK IS GUILTIER

I walk down to the hanging tree
to lean on the wind and cry
for dark babies without eyes
forever lost from me.

From the cotton fields I saw you,
puppets on a rope for a posse.
No one knew who was guilty
they hanged all three.

Two months and already the grass
erases your grave.
I hate the sun
that comes for me in the morning

I hate the corn growing
I hate the tree
that can live with you gone.

Reba Gloger

MISSING

Maidenhair, star-strangled
rooted in rock
cambering fans
a race of mountain water.

It fingers the cradled head.
Faceless the moon
taut on the tensiled skin
of the water

thins through the eye
of the night, bolts
past haunted woods
to escape, but is swallowed

by the mouth of the gorge.
Hounds nosing a cold trail,
ear leaning on the wind, wait.
They listen.

Reba Gloger

THE TEARS I SAVED

Liar . . . liar
you said forever,
never would you go away.
Today with hard tight knots
I tuck you into sails
and sink your boat.
Across the crying waters
your eyes float back.
Blind and scissored
by barnacles on the bottom
I taste your salty blood.

Reba Gloger

THE MESSENGER

Eagle-high on Sun Mountain
the deer
were in the velvet
and jackrabbits
lay frozen in the silence.

Mary Blackwing
was looking for firewood
under the pinons
when the Ancient of Days
spoke to her.

She came down from the mountain
sat all night by the kiva
turquoise squash-blossoms
blooming
around her throat.

Thistle soft
she told the moon
he comes
from the sun he comes.

Reba Gloger

THIS WAS WEATHER

That made you thankful.
Light flashed constantly—
fiends were racing the dimmers
on the light board.

A stagehand beat sheet metal,
and the wind had rhythm
like the seam in the wind machine drum
coming around and around
every two seconds.

The wife was thankful
the cat and dog were in
and the son home and in bed;
thankful not to be driving
or in a boat or
sleeping in a trailer.

The husband tripped
over the dog four times looking
for a candle and a match.
He said at least the oaks
are trimmed and we're not camping
like last week.

The son looked at the clock
and thought he might not
have to work tomorrow,
or only half a day.

Sally Hubbard

DAWN WATCH

Without looking up from my book
I know light has touched the neighbors' oaks.
I know how warm my husband is in our bed,
how strong and infinitely breakable children are,
how I leave behind daily what I need to carry
and take my worries everywhere,

How out of place I am in the city
needing to see farther than the back fence,
how gone my father is—not two years dead,
how good it is to find the kitchen clean—
knives and forks lined up in the drawer
in the morning.

SHUMARD OAK

Translucent
new green flecked with rust
soft with the hair of a young man's cheek,
without our looking
the first oak leaves have come,
not a half-inch long—but tomorrow
an inch, and fully green.
One leaf remains from last year
opaque
smooth
birth-red flecked with green.

Sally Hubbard

AT CHICHEN ITZA

We sat on random stones—carved fragments of columns—
under a shade tree and listened to the old guide tell
what his ancestors knew, what they built;
how the pyramid was designed so precisely
that in the night of the spring equinox
the notched shadow appears as a serpent undulating
down the facade to the great stone head below.

And the girl came close, listened, watched.
She was barefooted, clean, quiet and she carried
a mesh bag to fill with empty bottles
as the day burned on. The guide let her follow
to the huge ball court. She grinned for my camera
while he told of the rubber ball, the hoops,
the year-long games, the winning athletes
decapitated for the jaguar god.

We walked the cliffs circling the cenote—
the underground river with its muddy depths
of clay figues, gold and the bones of the purest girls;
the purifying steamhouse and diving stone unused
these thirteen centuries.

And she waited for us, chosen for sacrifice
the most proud, most pure, her role to be
a nameless mother of barefoot children,
not knowing the pleasure of a tub of clean water
or the freedom of reading and writing;
never going twenty miles from home, shapeless,
in an embroidered Mayan dress.

Sally Hubbard

COMING INTO LONDON

Outside
shinning tracks twist and separate
gliding by;
wires, poles, chimneys
share the cold.

Coal soot and smoke
add hours to the morning,
blur miles of tile roofs.
My mother's mother came from here,
from one of these endless flats.

Without warning I see straight
into undraped office windows:
twisted streamers looped
from light to light,
Chistmas cards taped to windowpanes.

I celebrate with you
and pass by, unknown,
as I knew glimpses
of my grandmother
and remained a stranger.

YOUNGEST BROTHER

From your sorrow to mine
a quilted sky stretches, white,
and geese cry.

Sally Hubbard

COWAN VALLEY

When we came to the mountain
we couldn't see it for the fog.

My father was out on the deck
trying to time the sunset—
just past four,
the shortest day of the year.
Cloud cancelled the valley,
made the closest tree limbs
loom up like buoys beckoning.

Somewhere in the house
there's a pastel of the valley—
one bare oak standing close by the cliff,
grey trees framing a stretched quilt
of pastures, winter wheat, sorghum fields;
a thin column of smoke rises up
from the cement plant chimney,
drifts over the ridge.
It must be forty years
since my father drew it.

They closed the plant this year.
And without my father
none of us can remember which trees
the sun will set between,
or what time.

Sally Hubbard

HOME FOR THE WEDDING

Like a pianist's hands
the Cumberland Plateau reaches
straight out, level,
then fingers bend and curve down
to the valley floor a thousand feet below,
where the farmland and towns
do not change.

Lights wink below at night
Like phosphorescence in a black boundless sea.

From the chancel's huge darkness
I watch my brother working
to control his hands, Bach,
and seventy-two ranks of pipes
for the marriage of our niece—
his face lit by the single console lamp,
his hair, changed, grey.

DECEMBER DIVORCE

Between fog clouds
the mountain's muscle and bone show
through the thin fabric of grey leaves,
bare trees stand separate
on the horizon,
and forgotten paths appear.

Sally Hubbard

STORY ROCK, COLORADO

It's so dry here. Gold, maroon, black kernels
cling to cobs of corn, and turkey feathers
still decorate bits of rough cotton cloth
tucked among pottery shards in one-room museums.

Under the streaked cliffs at Mesa Verde
my hands and feet fit in notches chipped in stone
nine hundred years ago.

I climb the rock walls wondering what gifts
the Anasazi have left in their honeycomb pueblos:
a handprint in the mortar between stones, my size;
and soot staining the corner where women cooked.

Above my head rock-hard nubs of beams mark upper rooms,
sleeping rooms, one ornamented with a blanket
painted in rust red zigzags on a smooth wall.

People not much different nine hundred years from now
will find evidence of us and know our simple needs
were the same, and leave their own story.

Ask the stars how small and continuing we are.
We bequeath ourselves by the work of our hands
in stone or paint or words—stick figures,
animals, unshucked corn etched on Story Rock.

Sally Hubbard

UKIYO-E

I always enter into it.
Somehow I issue out of my skin into the same
still violence of precise line and color
I watch now. Here there are no stars, it is a day
of storm. The arched, overwhelming curve of wave
fringed with stylized water and frothclawed foam
will drink in our bamboo boats as though they
were rice hulls skittering on a swirling sea.

Immediate as the experience of Zen: ten years
it has spent here stopped upon this wallwood,
another forty in the composition of my mind's
remembering, and centuries since
its original imaged conception.

Picture it: Fuji, faultless and serene
on the horizon—Hiroshige's floating world of cobalt
blue and white reachings, a wrathful wave poised for
all those years over slim boats—and our small figures
backbent, rowing, rowing.

Ukiyo-E translates from the Japanese as
floating world, *a realistic but highly imaginative*
painting style of the mid-Edo period, 1615-1868.

Mary Hurter

SNUGGLE UP

There must have been that first time
when you turned on your side
and I fit myself to your back—
knees up, like newborns together, breathing,
sleeping together breast to back,
belly to bottom, snuggled up.

We were newborns then, in those early days.
Our goals were simple: marriage, children,
useful work. We could not know
how much would depend on breast to back,
belly to bottom, snuggled up.

Once, your back to my front, you said—
Put your arms around me tight; we are going
for a ride. You revved up the engine loud,
and we zoomed away, laughing our heads
off to sleep, breast to back, belly to bottom, snuggled up.

Now as we settle for the night, it's—How
was your day? What did you do? And what
did they say?—to the tune of tired
bodies and aching bones. My dear, surely
you know—though I've always loved your front,
it's really your back that's taken us through
these thirty years—breast to back,
belly to bottom, all snuggled up.

Mary Hurter

SUBALPINE

Daybreak and thirty eight outside—
stacked log walls allow wide windows
open for white sound of the creek's free
versed creations, and the yellow of wild
canaries, wing-painting impressions across
crowds of alders that hid swift water.

Sensual delights of pinion and pine
flow in bareback in light come
silent over the mountain, carrying
the morning, soft and secret
as the owl who riffles evenings
down the canyon and closes each day.

Mary Hurter

THE BRIDGE

For a while you could not touch me.
I kept my thoughts within, shadowed
clouds of unknowing between you and me.
Your need was only tenpin thunder
in a Henry Hudson sky, bumping
around the mountains of my defense.

But then, surprised by your naked
rainstormed eyes, I see you clear,
fragile, warmed breath alive—
and know I must speak a bridge
across my protections, vulnerable
to the pain you will give like gold
at the end of this particular rainbow.

Mary Hurter

ASPHODEL,
YOU HAVE PLEASED
ME SINCE FIRST I KNEW
YOU. WHAT A NAME!
FLANNERY O'CONNOR LOVED YOU
IN HER WISE SORT OF WAY—POETS
HAVE ALWAYS USED YOU, AND EVEN I HAVE
ARGUED WITH MY HUSBAND FOR YEARS, TO
CARVE YOUR SYMBOLS IN THE GATEWOOD,
DEDICATE THE WHOLE TEN ACRES TO
THE SOUND AND SMOOTH
ASSONANTAL FEEL OF YOUR
NAME - A S P H O D E L.
STRANGE THAT
AN ARRANGEMENT OF
LETTERS, SYLLABLES
AND SOUNDS CAN BRING
SUCH PLEASURES TO
CURVED CONVOLUTIONS
OF THE MIND. SOME
DAY I HOPE TO MEET
YOU IN THE
PETAL.

Mary Hurter

PEARLY EVERLASTING

We labored all summer to put in this bed. Each chuff
of the shovel hit rocks that keep the mountains here
year after year, and with each push of our shoulders
and feet our lungs demanded more of the thin mountain
air, our sweat evaporated in the high dryness fast as
we produced it. Finally we opened earth

to the depth of eight inches all across the front, enough,
we congratulated ourselves, to take the flashy red
of Geraniums, though we knew they would not make
it through the winter. We began five days'
labor with the green wheelbarrow, banging down
to the creek full into the sharp cold flow

that will numb you in thirty seconds, legs aching with
the pain of it, heaving water-smoothed rocks, mottled
by age and composition, into the barrow, seven
or eight to the load. Then the grinding haul back,
one hundred fifty feet like one hundred miles, huffing,
dragging in rare air.

Stone by stone, their follow-the-leader-bordering sets
perimeters, discourages careless feet, anchors the cabin
onto ground. After two years of replanting store-boughts,
we gathered courage, shovel and wheelbarrow and went
for plants common to the land, down the mountain, all the
while thinking of our return, to clumps of spring-greened

spikes crowned by Fleur-de-lis in blue, named Iris by some
botanist who knew a goddess when he saw one, and groups of a gawky
stalky fur-stemmed white-petaled incongrosity, named by one
who must have been desperate for it—a pioneer perhaps, in these
same rocked mountains. It does last though, comes back
each year by its own strength and tenacity,

Mary Hurter

fills my bed and my mountain mind with whiteflowers
and dreamsongs, imaginings of a swirled, opalescent heaven
where I come to the garden alone while the dew is still
on the roses, of sunsets and moonrises in the gloaming,
of silver clouds, shimmering green fields, and bluebirds
of happiness in the sweet bye and bye whether or not it's true.

WEST BAY

Disturbed,
gulls rise in sheets
from the island
shimmering and moving
in the morning sun —
a southern borealis
in a daytime sky.

Mary Hurter

COLOR OF TIME AND SHAPE OF THINGS

The yellow morning
bit the sun into squares
of sunlight reflecting
a watercolor project

laid out — pinned in place
orange incandescence
last night's efforts
now an impotent pink.

Lunch in the garden
blue and white cloth laid out
and pinned in place by
cranberry glass, chartreuse

melon — the usual conversation,
inflation   Reagan   and pollution.

Lucille Joy

STILL LIFE

for Dorothy Fournier

I know not to move
When lights float the river
Bringing a kind of happiness
Bending the dry grass of summer
That strays from its roots

The stars are out early
And the moon in West Texas
Knows the road the wind
Takes along the Guadalupe
On such a night without rain

You tell me again nothing is real
As you arrange wildflowers
At the sliced edge of the river
Trembling in the liquid flow of shadow
They will bloom in tomorrow's still life

Lucille Joy

VARIATIONS ON A TEXT BY DONALD JUSTICE

I will die in Houston in the heat,
On a day when the humidity is high,
A day like all the other days,
A day that no one is aware of yet,
And the dampness will fog glasses
Of the few friends and relatives,
And children I have not seen for months;
Then they will take me to Alice,
Where all will drive slowly because now
There is time to speak softly of regret.

I think it will be on a Monday like today,
But the air will be dry and no rain expected,
Winds from the Gulf of Mexico will stir the dust.
This day the South Texas sky will be heavy
With thunder, as unfamiliar as this family
From Houston standing alone in the dry lot,
Where Mexican grave diggers will curse,
As they shovel the hard clods of earth,
But not too loudly, out of respect,
As my husband will be taking his nap.

Lucille Joy is dead. One day the rain started
To fall, and cars moved down the road slowly,
Because of the smell of the storm,
Then one of the diggers pushed his spade
In the hard earth and cursed
As another crossed himself, saying, "Santa Maria",
As the rain clouds rolled over,
And the wind blew the clods
That fell on my coffin,
And it sounded like rain . . .

Lucille Joy

THE LANGUAGE OF WINTER

Inside we live
In a candlelit, apple wood world,
While through my study window

I watch the shrubs shiver,
Squat and leafless
As the north wind moves

Into a human language,
Berating the loose shingle.
Thin birds turning on wired ice

Are made frantic by wind chimes;
Tones tossed to exhaustion
Still ring a posthumous warning

To the limp Swedish ivy
Trailing a consolatory finger,
Pointing directly to

Unsolved winter language:
The bone ache shriek of wind.
Then the snow-whisper of covering up.

I try to remember that wine
Will follow the tasteless wafer
If we live long enough to accept.

Lucille Joy

DAHLIAS SPARROWS AND WIND

It is a small room
With stale air,
Too small for long conversation.
We push against bare walls
Trying to avoid the dead zinnias.

We have left our breath outside
In a parking lot with our car —
With the motor still running.
Brusque figures move in and out
Of the silence, their hands hurt
from duty and ammonia.

I bring my daughter back from death:
Her laughter erases the room
I am in, and we are back in our garden
Of dahlias, sparrows and wind.
Her long hair flies like a scarf
Behind her — I open my arms.

Near by, a hoarse voice
Reminds me it is time
To leave it all behind us.
Out in the crisp autumn air,
I know if I had it to do over again,
I would do it over again.

Lucille Joy

THE SASANQUA TREE

It is October through my window
and the Sasanqua tree is blooming,
pale pink snow dancing on the tips
of a slate green throne. Planted
in your honor, while you were in Japan
fighting World War Two.
Your first wife burned
her body waiting at the same window,
alone, while you marched
without real guns, with men
in dull costumes; hardly a uniform
described the shape of a soldier.

Years later you told me every morning
at breakfast, how when you were in Manila
you stepped over dead Japs, bloated
by the roadside, waiting for their dark
and perfect women, like your perfect wife
waiting under the Sasanqua in your garden.
You are not leaving your place,
a nest with her feathers still clinging,
though the hungry, small birds have flown;
and I with my own grown children,
visiting them only in dreams,
have at last won the prize.

We rake the dry leaves together,
to pile on your first wife's mulch bed,
where she asked to be buried.
But she is certainly not there —
you can hear her singing from the
throat of that mockingbird;
clear and free, she sings from the top
of the Sasanqua tree in our garden.

Lucille Joy

NIGHT REFLECTIONS

Lights of the night, on an all night trip
to Mexico, transform the unplanted fields,
where Spanish ponies once grazed, lowering
proud heads to the stunted chaparral,
searching for the blue grass and clear water,
only to nuzzle the dead roots of cedars,
hacked to their knees by the Mexican cowboys
my father had once hired.

We pass through my home town, near the border,
and again I am only five, half asleep on the back seat.
I hear the noisy engine of our old Hudson touring car,
that rocks me when the tires fit the ruts
on lonely dirt roads. I hold the reflection
of my father's face in the dim light of the dashboard
when we stop long enough for a gate to be opened,
then back to the black night lit by moon light,
and flares from tired oil wells, exposing
an abandoned building that seems to lean in on me.

The moon, racing beside us, is cracked by bare
branches of the mesquite trees, and tonight
I still hear the howl, or was it a cry —
from one lone coyote, off in that brush somewhere.

Lucille Joy

ASSERTION

I am no scholar in the ways of love,
Nor skilled in it except as mind's pale structure
Patterned after some bookish architecture,
Nor have I often practiced how to move
This way or that, beneath, around, above,
Having found wanting each pedantic lecture,
Each stew of hearsay but a sorry mixture
Of curiosities I could not prove
Granted my interest — yet having ample
Wit for firm flesh, its sinewy strategem
Of eye and ear, of nose and mouth, am ready
To taste your weary sweat, to take the simple
Test of your pulse with mine, kiss your sweet stem,
So bearing off the prizes in such study!

Vassar Miller

THE TEMPTATION

When Jesus fast went fasting into the
wilderness, he grew so famished till
the devil came to him and said, "If
you are the Son of God make these stones into
bread." but Jesus, knowing somehow
that He Himself that He was the real bread, said, "No
one lives by bread alone, but by each
word come from the mouth of God." and blew the devil
off with golden breath for a moment, but
the devil came back and said, "If you
are the Son of God, jump down from these rocks high
as the temple towers, and, who knows, maybe
the angels will catch you!" Jesus looked down to
the desert floor stretching beneath Him long
as His thirst has been, dry as His throat would ever
be until at last death took it, shuddering
said, "You must not tempt the Lord, your God." and
spat the devil off His tongue until His
foe bit back at Him, "If You are the Son of
God, be wise. Fall down, then, and worship
Me!" and Jesus, empty-handed, stripped to
bear the hot whip of the sun without one
more word, turned His back on the devil who
left Him for a little, long enough till
wild beasts could come lick His sore feet like angels.

Vassar Miller

BELATED THANKS

My body, derided and driven
before the thin lash of thought,
I confess it is you, only you —

eyes, undefended and fragile,
stationed upon you frontier,
bearing the twinkle of leaves on the wind;

ears, such lopsided patens
holding bells and birdsong and laughter,
pure eucharists of all sound;

skin scribbled over and over
with roses and mud and warm baths,
the signatures of the earth;

brain, compressing the eons
from ape-man to astronaut
in a sphere looking much like an orange:

from comet to atom—every blossom
of breath, the whole startle of wonder
leans on your lurching shoulders.

Vassar Miller

OBLATION

I kneel,
my heart in my hands—
a cold fish,
a stale loaf.

What are
these among so many?
Lord, Your business
is to know.

I rise,
my body a shell
heavy with
emptiness,

You whom
worlds cannot contain
not disturbing
one pulse beat.

My bones
being boughs aflame
with Thy glory,
Lord, suffices.

Vassar Miller

BIOGRAPHY

She lived
each day, dying an inch each night,
and lived again

each day
longer and longer till, one night,
swallowed by yards,
the stitch
of pear bloom vanished, wound upon
the spool of night.

Vassar Miller

LOVE

like a child
lies nameless
ignorant
laughter
like a child
lies shameless
nimblefoot
cripple
like a child
laid wound wrong when
no conning can tell you
like a child
lay down long in
the dumbness
of prayer.

MEDITATION

Ah, oh, om, ha, home, go home, old
woman where there is no home — where no
one is home, where all are home where every
one is home, come home when no one seems
at home, when every one seems gone,
run to a hole in the ground, hum, ho and
hum, hum ah, om, ho, home, till some
dog summons to the corporal works of mercy.

Vassar Miller

DEAR FRIENDS

Today I am fine
because it is March the First
and I am moving on over to Easy Street
although I have had that for a secret address all along
but it is not an easy one to remember
except for the curs
and the wild bulls of Bashan
who number the bones of the rich
and lick up their asses
and curry the favor
from the ripe mouths of poets
those artists
most like the Lord God
who created the worlds out of nothing
but the breath of His mouth
so the singer may sing
but her mouth shall soon run with the spittle of worms
and the dancer may dance
but the dogs of death
that nip at his heels
will soon run him down
so the sculptor may sculpt
and the artist may build
but time has planted its bomb
beneath the foundation of every one of their works
and its thumb presses hard on the trigger
while the poet weaves her shimmering webs of saliva
over the hard-driven face of the universe.

Vassar Miller

TALKING

A painted kitchen table covered with oilcloth—
a criss-cross pattern of yellow and green,
nothing special. Only it is.
It's where they like to sit,
My father and my grandfather,
while a summer evening eases into night,
poking their spoons into glasses
of crackers and milk, pointing
the spoons as they talk, intent
as checker players who've long since
known each other's moves by heart.

They never agree about Roosevelt or God,
but it doesn't seem to matter
because the table joins them,
as it always has. What matters
is the talk, that they love it,
that they hold the words and sentences
like treasures, turn them
into music I keep listening to
when it stops, into small bursts
of fireworks I keep watching
after they fall.

Cathy Stern

FEBRUARY COMPLAINT, HOUSTON

Winter can turn against you now:
days right out of April, and you're not ready;
sun like a feather drawn down the skin;
the smell of fresh turned earth, and lilacs,
blown in from God knows where.
You have to close the fireplace flue,
maybe for a week.
You have to be careful.
Don't stay in bed, for example,
or cry, unless you can explain.
If you must go to the supermarket,
lean on the cart.
Leave the mail unopened and breathe deeply.
Remember only what you can forget.
Never mind that your mother said,
Still says, often repeats:
no one should live on weather,
even here.

Especially here.

Cathy Stern

REVELATION

I could say it was
the way sunlight entered
the twelve-paned window,
fell onto the varnished floor
in slanted squares,
faint dust riding its beams
down into shadow, vanishing.

That first moment
when the breath stops short
of stopping, the wrapper
ripped from the emptiness
you don't want to know about
and never will
until it's yours.

A weight carried back
of the brain each day,
back into the brain each night,
the parallel darkness
promising release
if you will let go of now
now, as you will have to then.

Cathy Stern

SWIMMING IN THE GULF AT FIFTY

Going out, I never think about dying.
Or maybe I always do. I concentrate
on sand moving under my feet,
on the rush of rising water,
how it touches my skin—insistent
as a lover's hand.
The deeper waves have their own compulsions.
I give in to the lift and fall
until, out past the breakers,
I lie down in the slow swell
and everything glides away.

But this time, coming back,
the hidden currents found me out.
I swam minute after minute
in the same deep spot,
held in the heavy motion
of the waves. My arms ached
with water, my breath became water,
water drew me down and whispered:
this is when they let go.
Before my foot touched the ground,
I saw my hair turn to seaweed on the foam.

Cathy Stern

DRIVING BACK FROM THE COUNTRY ON SUNDAY

Perhaps it's the ritual of leaving
that place, the closing up of the cabin,
the locking of the gate, the turning
into the narrow black-top road—
something in us changes

when that slanted light is on the fields
at five in the afternoon, that fallen
light, inward and luminous, unlike
the fresh sun of mornings there
that opens up the landscape,

when that darkness starts on the gound, under
the long lines of trees bordering
the pastures, and white cows
glow in the pale green of those fields,
white cow birds at their feet,

when that road rolls over the stretched
shadows of water oaks and cedars,
by farmhouses and tin-roofed
barns, black ponds and wire fences,
and nameless field flowers,

and we know we do not move,
that all sound has left the turning earth,
that the silent land moves
past us, an old film
we run over and over and over.

Cathy Stern

LOVE POEM

It would be hard to say when I first sensed

the change, noticed myself watching you
again, as you swept the floor, or as you rinsed
the dishes—you knowing how I hate to do
most domestic things;
                                        harder still to decide
when the sudden waves of tenderness
returned—you lying there, as always, beside
me, touching my arm before sleep, a caress
so ordinary, so familiar as
to be too dull for books;
                                             hardest of all
now, to know how to speak of it—how it has
changed and changed between us, how the small
things have become the largest—how an old promise
turns, becomes new.
                                      But you know all this.

Cathy Stern

A CABIN IN ROLLING COUNTRY: A STILL LIFE FOR MY FATHER

It's not as rough as New Hampshire here.
Old roads are scarce, and none as old
as the one you took me down each summer
as if for the first time. The wagon ruts,
almost overgrown, started back
of Goss's barn and went on forever,
always stretching ahead of us, always
sun on the weeds and clouds of gnats
whirling in the thin light.
The road dropped sharply into dark woods
and climbed out over fields of boulders,
and then we'd find the cellar holes
again, their crumbled chimneys rising
above the stilled ground, strange
monuments in a bright wind, indecipherable.

This morning, nothing is really different.
You died years before I bought this place
and are buried half a continent away.
Perhaps it's just an oddity of light,
fragile as memory, that's fallen pale
in shards through the layered branches
of water oaks, and shattered in the grass,
or the way the window has suddenly
framed the familiar, lifted it
out of time into perfect stillness:
the clearing in the woods beyond
the small ravine, the footbridge
that crosses over. I go there
each time I come here—sometimes farther,
into the tangle of brush and trees.

But, not now. For this moment,
it's a place past entering in the flesh,
flat as it is, without depth,
yet the distance has no end while
I take you there.

Cathy Stern

MILKING TIME

Black-haired Clem and black-and-white Flore
drive the cows to the barn
from the bottom land pasture.

The cows affect not to see them,
pretend it's their own idea to move,
a few steps at a time.

They're ungainly, huge, red with white fronts.
Who, me? they seem to say
and low their resentment

but enter with dignity by ones
and twos at the cow barn door
and go into their stanchions.

Clem attaches the teat cups to each
swelling udder. Peace comes to the barn
as he pulls the switch,

a quiet filled with the pulse
of the machine—squeeze and suck,
squeeze and suck. Clem smiles.

He puts a fresh stick of gum in his mouth,
does the final stripping by hand.
He fills pails with the white froth,

carries them into the separator room—
clean, cold, wet, stone.
Calves and kittens get the skim.

Helen Williams

THE FISH

Fish have nothing much in common with music,
except scales. It's water that makes melodies,
while fish in enigmatic beauty merely swim,
with waving tails
or hover motionless, lead-colored, nosing weeds,
unaware they bear the shape of fear.

Father, Grandfather,
the fish have eaten what you left for me,
a ribbon printed with words.
I dream I am unwrapping fish, the skin, the flesh,
I dream of surgery on fish.

But once, as usual underwater in disgrace,
I dived more deeply down into the murk.
The water promptly drained away and I was
high upon a sunny coast, and somewhere,
shrill and clear, the fish were singing.

Helen Williams

I CAN DRAW ROSES

We burned logs in the grate
once or twice this year, a mild winter,
stared into the heart of the fire
where the live coals glowed the color of roses—
Tropicanas, Mojaves.
But now it's the season of ashes.
The roses took root in the heart
but they bloomed into ashes.
The thorns are at large
and I'm stuck in this grey-and-white movie
without any compass,
walking, without much conviction, the powdery fields,
haunting the open,
courting the shafts
with my pen at the ready, thinking
if some stray arrow
should draw blood the color of roses,
or if I should draw roses,
I would be out of this,
home in the sun and dreaming of summer.

Helen Williams

THE KASHGAR

I saw her in an underground bazaar
where grapes and melons, pomegranates gleamed
with all the sun's absorbed power, bolts
of cobweb silk, gold in the border, glowed
blue, mulberry. She wore the same
in gold-edged flounces, a swordflash in her smile.

Then in the sun I saw her life—
of men, and animals, and rope—I saw it
strung calligraphy across the brown plain,
the straight backs riding at ease in the dusty pall,
and in the midst, the skirts outspread sidesaddle
glinting with gold. As if from outside time
the ancient, intricately patterned scroll unrolled
before my eyes, and then it rolled away.

Helen Williams

AT SCHOOL

Lorraine, Lorraine,
I marked you down
for your black-rimmed nails,
and never listened to you tell

the reason—"It's all those pans—"
the dirty pans you had to clean.
I was a prig; the teacher made
me neatness-checker of fourth grade.

Thank God I didn't get all righteous
when you used my plot in English class.
It was a bummer—not original with me.
But teacher pounced and you looked down so humbly.

Every fall you missed weeks
plucking turkeys for your folks
in a shack off the county road.
And I bet you never got paid.

O Lorraine, with your bush of hair,
your purple sweater,
your everlasting chewing gum,
you ran off with a traveling salesman,

came back in a neat green suit,
a pretty haircut,
eyes remote as clay.
In custody.

Lorraine, Lorraine,
my world has gone
to dust. And I was dumb
until I said your name.

Helen Williams

MY MOTHER WORE DIAMONDS

The train comes by in the night
with its load of tin thunder,
its klaxon sounding a major sixth
with an odd maternal effect.

Mother wore sapphires and diamonds
on black velvet,
she was doing the clasp that day
a cousin so tormented me

I came for comfort, and she put me out.
And the sun turned black in the sky.
But my glimpse of her stayed with me,
a feeling of something about to happen

in her reined-in walk,
the pendant shifting,
settling on her breast,
the diamonds pointing at her heart.

Tonight, as the train sounds fade,
my mother's necklace
comes rattling out of the sky
and hangs at my eyes.

Helen Williams

CLIMB

At the beginning we were puzzled.
He did not seem like the right sort of guide.
And it did not seem like the right sort of mountain.
Yet we felt somehow it was the only mountain; and he,
taciturn, failing to meet our eyes,
at times disappearing altogether, was its guide.
So, when he began to climb, quietly,
without preliminaries, we followed.
He seemed to us always to ask for nothing,
not even to be understood. But we followed.
It was difficult going. He stopped where there were hardly stances,
brought us up short at impossible pitches.
Yet each time the impasse was turned, turned easily,
he did it without effort when he was ready,
and we came out onto a safe place where we could look down,
at the blurred, faraway villages of the plain.
And so we came to feel the rhythm of the mountain,
and of our ascent, and to know the quality of our guide.
And when we got close to the top, we rose
on a shrill burst of energy like the wind from the top,
exploding out of the mutings, the constraints
of the climb, and of our doubts. The bald bare summit.
At this moment, when there was nothing but sky before us,
and what we had done humbled, appalled us
even as we felt released like the arrow from the bow,
we found our guide had disappeared again.
We came back down the mountain without him.

Helen Williams

ABOUT THE POETS

V.T. ABERCROMBIE is a sculptor, poet, co-author of three catering books for the Houston area, the latest being CATERING TO HOUSTON; and co-editor, CHRISTMAS IN TEXAS, an anthology of poems on the Christmas theme.

MAE S. BARCLAY, a native of Louisiana, is an industrial designer, artist and sculptor. She lived in South America and Mexico for many years, and owns an advertising/public relations firm in Houston.

SIMONE BATEMAN, born in France, lived many years in South America, but this last twenty years has been polishing her English in Houston.

MARY ESTHER BINTLIFF has had her poems published in *The Texas Quarterly, Quartet, The Forum, Travois, An Anthology of Texas Poetry,* and *Christmas in Texas.* She paints, sculpts, lives in Austin, Texas.

ELIZABETH BRATTEN is a native of Savannah, Georgia. After completing her education in nursing, she married and moved to Texas and has lived in Houston the greater part of her life. Member of a poetry workshop since 1974, she is completing her degree in English at the University of Houston.

MARY LOUISE FERGUSON says that she is married to the last of the oldtime cowboys, who is also a geophysicist, and many of her poems come from their days in various "hometowns" across the country. She now lives in the Hempstead/Brenham area and attends a class at A&M. Her poems have been published in several *Books of the Year,* Poetry Society of Texas; *South & West;* University of Houston anthology, *Hippocrene;* and the anthology *Christmas in Texas.*

REBA GLOGER was born on the prairie near Galveston and has lived on ranches most of her life. Now living in Santa Fe, she is continuing her painting, sculpture, and writing.

SALLY HUBBARD, a native of Tennessee, attended Sweet Briar College and Tulane University, and has lived in Houston nine years. She was chosen to read her poems at the Houston Festival in 1982 and has won prizes from the Poetry Society of Texas, Houston division, 1983. She has been a soprano in the Concert Choir of New Orleans and the Houston Symphony Chorale.

MARY HURTER spent her childhood in the deep woods of the Brazos River bottomlands. Her major interests besides her family are theology, philosophy, and psychology. She has held a variety of positions in American Friends Service International.

VASSAR MILLER, born, reared, and educated in Houston, is the author of six books of poetry—*Adam's Footprint, Wage War on Silence, My Bones Being Wiser, Onions and Roses, If I Could Sleep Deeply Enough,* and *New and Selected Poems;* and two chapbooks, *Small change* and *Approaching Nada.* She is a former Poet Laureate of Texas.

LUCILLE JOY is a portrait painter and is married to Houston portrait artist Robert Joy. She has been writing poetry for eight years. Her work has been published in *The Texas Quarterly, The Forum, Domestic Crude,* and *Christmas in Texas.* She was chosen to read during the Houston Festival at the Houston Public Library and at Tranquillity Park.

CATHY STERN is a graduate student and teaching assistant in English at the University of Houston.

HELEN WILLIAMS, North Dakota-born, went to Vassar and worked then and later as a reporter, editor, and publicist. She has lived in Houston for 29 years, co-edited *Christmas in Texas.* She plays the piano, prefers Bach.